Prince Ragnal, ar holiday ver:

Eleanor C. Donnelly

Alpha Editions

This edition published in 2024

ISBN 9789362090775

Design and Setting By

Alpha Editions
www.alphaedis.com

Email - info@alphaedis.com

As per information held with us this book is in Public Domain.
This book is a reproduction of an important historical work.
Alpha Editions uses the best technology to reproduce historical work
in the same manner it was first published to preserve its original nature.
Any marks or number seen are left intentionally to preserve.

Contents

THE EVE.	- 1 -
THE DAWN.	- 5 -
THE PERFECT DAY.	- 9 -
Christmas Carol.	- 13 -
At Dame Noël's.	- 16 -
A Murillo.	- 20 -
The Stable of Bethlehem.	- 22 -
The Three Masses on Christmas Day.	- 24 -
The God-Man.	- 26 -
Bethlehem's Queen.	- 27 -

THE EVE.

White and chill from the wintry skies,
The starlight falls upon ancient Eire:
The wind makes moan thro' the leafless trees
Of Devenish Isle, like a soul in fear,—
Deep in the heart of its snowy woods,
Fanning a peat-flame, lone and drear.

The ruined hut where that turf-fire glows
Hath never a roof of thatch or stone,
But bow and spear on the rude walls hang,
And a bed of skins on the floor is strewn,
Where, close to the embers, stern and still,
Ragnal the leper sits alone.

Ragnal of Errigal, prince of doom,
His face, a death-mask of despair;—
The foul disorder's loathly scales
Lacquer his skin with their hideous glair:
Dulling the blue of his brave young eye,
Dimming the gold of his tangled hair.

Bowed like a churl of three-score ten,
His peakéd chin in his wasted hands,
He watches the flames with a sluggish eye,
Sparkle and glow in their fiery dance;
Till, deep in the embers, pictured, lie
His life's lost hopes—its dead romance.

A royal castle beside the sea,
On breezy cliffs, exultant, set:
A Prince and Princess, young and fair,
Pacing the grassy parapet,
The golden fringe of his long, bright hair
Sweeping the maiden's locks of jet.

Thro' perfum'd air, replete with peace,
The swallows skim the blue waves' flow:
The lovely Dympna's hand, at rest
On her lover's arm (a thing of snow)—
Thrills, as he bends his head, and breathes
In her blushing ear, a whisper low.

She gathers the fleece of her floating veil
From the nodding shade of his raven plume,
As, gravely pleading, he bends again
To hear those bright lips speak his doom.
—Why does she start and lift her head?
Why are her cheeks devoid of bloom?

He sees the flash of her wide, dark eye,
He hears her clear voice rise and fall:
"Sooner than sell my faith in Christ,
My life I'd yield—my love—my all!
Content my bridal vows should prove
A martyr's grave and a virgin's pall!"

Then, in the flames, his other self
He sees, erect in scorn and pride:
"Sooner would I a leper be,
Far from the world to crouch and hide,
Than bend to a Christian priest mine knee,
Or take to mine arms a Christian bride!"

The royal blood leaps in her face,
Her voice rings out its golden knell:
"O Christ! incline Thy pitying grace,
And pardon this poor infidel!"
Then, with averted, shuddering gaze,
"Unhappy Ragnal! fare thee well!"

A sudden darkness shuts her in ...
The flutter of her snowy gown—
The sunlit towers—the sparkling waves
In pallid embers, crumble down;
As Ragnal by the fire sits,
A leprous Prince without a crown!

"O lily, nurtured by the sea!
Sweet Dympna, long-lost, promised bride!
Thine unknown Christ"—(he cries aloud):
"This night hath triumph'd o'er my pride!
Forgive me!"—Lo! a gust of song
Fills all the wintry world outside!

THE DAWN.

A thrilling, heavenly harmony
From silvern harps and lutes divine:
The Leper, prostrate on his face,
Drinks in the glorious draught like wine;
Then, rising, reels like drunken wight,
Into the starlight's wondrous shine.

For strange, unearthly lustres fill
The frosty air. To Ragnal blown,
Across Lough Erne, there comes the breath
Of sweetest blossoms ever grown;
Yet, right or left, above, below,
No living thing or shape is shown.

All wordless, o'er the sparkling Lough,
The music steals again—but hark!
"*Gloria in excelsis!*" sings
A voice, up-soaring like a lark;
While: "*Et in terra pax!*" (strange words!)
Drop down to Ragnal thro' the dark.

His breast heaves with a mighty fear,
The strong man trembles like a reed:
The while the minstrels float before,
(Tho' ulcer'd feet and ankles bleed),
Straight onward through the shining wood,
He needs must follow where they lead;

And walks, and walks, and walks, and walks,
His bare feet buried in the snow;
While flaming eyes of savage beasts
From bog and thicket, glare and glow.
He sees the stars slide down the east,
He hears the cocks begin to crow.

Yet walks, and walks, and walks, and walks,
Till ev'ry nerve and sinew aches,
And sweat and blood and loathly scales
Mark ev'ry painful step he takes—
When, suddenly, the rapturous sound
That lured him on—his path forsakes!

And with his burning forehead bared,
The hoar-frost on his yellow locks,
The Leper finds himself before
An open cave, wherein an ox
And ass are stalled—dumb, placid brutes,—
Their manger rooted in the rocks.

And in the midst—O Vision strange!—
A Woman glorious as the moon,
Upon whose breast, a radiant Child
Lies, like a rosebud blown in June,
His eyes (twin-lamps of Paradise!)
Making the night a brilliant noon.

They look on Ragnal sweet, yet sad,
And Ragnal bends his aching knee;
He stretches forth his wasted arms,
And cries: "Eternal praise to Thee!
O Blessed Christ! Thine hour is come—
Complete the work begun in me!"

    And then, he swoons—how long—how short
      A space, he knows not—till his eyes
        He, languid, opens to the dawn,
      Faint-blushing in the eastern skies;
       And sees the cavern full of shapes,
       And blazing with a glad surprise!

THE PERFECT DAY.

An altar cloth'd with pure samite,
Adorned with gold and precious stones—
A Christian priest in vestments white
Baptizing many little ones;
And all the people on their knees
Singing in full, melodious tones!—

Whose hand on Ragnal's shoulder lies?
Whose sweet voice murmurs in his ear?
"For such as *thou*, the Christ was born;
Arise, Prince Ragnal, and draw near!"
A veiléd woman leads him down
To where the altar-lights shine clear.

The Hidden Presence strong and sweet
His erring son would closer draw.
In the warm glory of the shrine,
His icy blood begins to thaw:
Yet Ragnal dare not lift his eyes—
He trembles with delicious awe.

What time the children yield him place,
(Without a look or sign of dread),
Kneeling before the agéd priest,
The sacred words are softly said;
And with a thrill of joy, he feels
The saving waters on his head.

O miracle of purest faith!
The people shout and clap their hands—
Like some foul mantle, earthward, cast,
Down drop the Leper's loathsome bands!—
Ragnal, the Golden-hair'd, once more,
In manly beauty, perfect, stands!

While, clear and strong to Heaven's high court,
Goes up the glorious Christmas hymn—
The shrouded woman at his side
Flings back her veil from eyes that swim
With happy tears—and DYMPNA'S face
Shines star-like, from the shadows dim!

Forgiven the past—forgot the pains
Which made *that* face his bitterest dream;
A trusting smile is on its lips,
Its eyes with glad affection beam,
While, down the Prince's waving beard,
The grateful tears, unbidden, stream.

The priest hath joined their willing hands;
The day grows bright—the wind blows free—
As thro' the woods, they go to seek
Their sunlit castle by the sea.
O Ragnal of the Golden Hair!
The Lord hath gracious dealt with thee!

And in the midst—O Vision strange!—
A Woman glorious as the moon,
Upon whose breast, a radiant Child
Lies, like a rosebud blown in June.

Christmas Carol.

I.

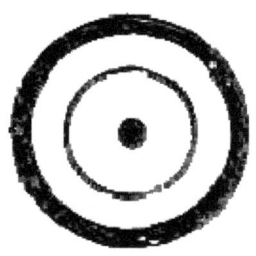

O holy Night! O starry Night,
That ushers in Salvation's morn!
O blessed Eve of rare delight,
Whereon the Christ was born!
Thine angels flood the hills with song,
And rouse the shepherds from their sleep;
While past'ral pipes the lay prolong,
Around the Stable door, they throng
With votive lambs and sheep.

Sing *Gloria*, sing *Gloria*
In excelsis Deo!

II.

O solemn Night! O lustrous Night,
That fills the earth with brightest Day!
The Wise Men come in robes of white
From kingdoms far away.

What time their weary journey ends,
They haste to worship Judah's King;

In jewel'd zones and bazubends
Behold the three Chaldean friends,
Gold, myrrh, and incense bring!

   Sing *Gloria*, sing *Gloria*
   In excelsis Deo!

III.

O radiant Night! O Night of nights!
Thy bells ring sweet from Paradise;
Thine orient Star, eternal, lights
   The Crib where Jesus lies!
Wealth of the poor, the mourner's joy,
The sinner's shield, the captive's hope,
This Babe—the Virgin's sinless Boy—
Shall sin and hell and death destroy,
   And heaven's portals ope!

   Sing *Gloria*, sing *Gloria*
   In excelsis Deo!

*This Babe—the Virgin's sinless Boy—
Shall sin and hell and death destroy,
And heaven's portals ope!*

(See page 25.)

At Dame Noël's.

AN OLD-WORLD TRADITION.

The clock strikes Twelve! 'Tis Christmas Eve
At old Dame Noël's farm;
Beyond the house, with holly wreathed,
The barn in mistletoe is sheathed.
(God save us from all harm!)

The red cock to the manger springs,
And shrills its Christmas prayer;
Three times, it flaps its shining wings,
Then, "*Christus—natus—est!*"—it sings.
—The ox roars "*Ubi?*—Where?"

But, soft thro' swaths of sun-dried grass,
It hears the lamb below,
From out the shimmering, scented mass,
Bleat: "*Beth'lem! Beth'lem!*"—Brays the ass:
"*Eamus!*—Let us go!"

And 'round about the hive (whose zone
    Shall summer sweets embalm),
The bees go floating as they drone,
Go floating, as they thus intone
    Their honeyed, midnight psalm:

"Let all Creation praise the Lord,
Who comes to men this Christmas morn:
The Son of God, th' Incarnate Word,
    In Bethlehem of Mary born!

"Good ox, good ass, your brothers wait
This hour beside His Crib—A sign
There, too, is thine, meek lamb; thy Mate
    Is Blessed Mary's Lamb divine!

"And, from thy seed, bold Chanticleer!
Shall spring that bird of Passiontide,
Whose voice shall thrice to Peter's ear

Proclaim: 'Thou hast thy Lord denied!'

"*Ah! tho' we little bees may ne'er
Find in the Holy Babe, our part;
Nor, with our sweetest honey, dare
To heal His tender, bleeding heart;*

"*Tho' none of us may share Man's grace,
Nor claim his Saviour newly-born,
Yet do we still His mercies praise,
And bless His birth, this Christmas morn!*"

Thus do the bonny creatures strive
To hail Love's mystery;
In comely shapes, alert, alive,
Thus do they greet, in stall and hive,
Our Lord's Nativity!

Thus, do the Soulless keep the feast
At old Dame Noël's farm;

The Christmas star shines in the east,
Soft chimes the bell—swift glides the priest—
God save us from all harm!

A Murillo.

The lovely Christ-Child, like a lily, lies
Within His Maiden Mother's pure embrace—
The azure depths of her adoring eyes,
The faithful mirrors of His glorious face!

The while upon her bosom, warm and white,
She shelters Him, with love and tender awe,
From the bleak darkness of the winter night,
From the rough manger and the bristling straw,

The shepherds at the dazzling Vision stare;
The gentle beasts, at Joseph's touch, bow down;
And angel choirs in vibrant tones declare
That Christ is born a babe in David's town!

O Babyhood, the harbinger of hope
To every babe enthroned on woman's breast!
O Motherhood, within whose gracious scope

All lesser motherhood is shrined and blessed!

No sceptred Cæsar can dispute *your* sway—
Angels or men your golden mission claim—
For yours is Christ—to-day and yesterday,
And thro' the eternal ages, still the same!

The Stable of Bethlehem.

There is no ante-chamber in this royal palace,
There are no waiting-rooms of haughty state:
No chamberlain austere, no courtiers puff'd with malice,
To shut us out from where the King doth wait—
The new-born King, unscepter'd and uncrown'd,
In swaddling-bands of lowly linen bound.

Open and wide to all, are these old palace-portals—
The very beasts have found their way therein.
Amid the thronging Angels, would ye seek for mortals?
Behold the Virgin without stain of sin,
And Joseph, her chaste spouse!—Thrice belssèd pair!
They kneel before the Babe in wordless prayer!

The sweetest, fairest Babe e'er seen! Thro' ruined rafters,
The happy stars shine in upon His stall;
The keen wind, blowing from the fields and mountain-pastures,
Deepens the rose-tint of His visage small,
And bids His hands, on Mary's bosom, glow
Like soft, pink blossoms on a drift of snow.

Kneel and adore Him! Bring your hearts, as stainless lilies,
To cast before His darling, dimpled feet!
Soon shall the shepherds from the dusky hills and valleys,
In simple faith, around His manger meet;
And stately Kings, on wondrous quest intent,
Shall bring their gifts from out the Orient.

O Love, so free, so royal, yet so condescending—
So unpretentious in Thy majesty!
As Thy beginning, even so shall be Thine ending
Upon the open heights of Calvary!
A fountain, free to all beneath God's heaven,
Wherein all sinners may be cleansed and shriven!

Here is the well-spring of those sparkling, saving waters—
Here, in the heart of Mary's Blessed Boy!
From out the Saviour's fountains, O earth's sons and daughters,
Ye shall draw graces with exceeding joy;
And, with the Christmas Angels, rapturous, sing:
Glory and homage to the new-born King!

The Three Masses on Christmas Day.

I.

"The Lord hath said to me: Thou art my Son, this day have I begotten thee."—Ps. ii, 7.

Deep in the bosom of the Father lies
His co-eternal Word—the Infinite,
Whose generation's everlasting light
Illumes the unborn ages.... Lift your eyes,
And contemplate that Home in Paradise,
That first eternal Dwelling of the Word!—
Before the angels were,—before the skies
Blush'd over Eden, or the waters stirred
Under the Spirit's strong, creative breath,—
Uttered the Father in His bosom blest
This glorious Word.... What matter change or death?
Amid the Godhead's central fires expressed,
Life lives in Love.—O men of vision dim,
Here, at His altars, kneel, and worship Him!

II.

"And they came with haste, and they found Mary and Joseph, and the Infant lying in a manger."—Luke ii, 16.

Tho' midnight shadows wrap Him in their pall,
The stars upon His rosy sweetness shine;
From Mary's bosom to the cattle-stall,
He passes in His baby grace divine!
Venite adoremus. In this shrine,

Our God appears, our Saviour, and our All!
Before the Word made Flesh, adoring, fall,
And praise the Everlasting's blest design.
Far, o'er the hills, the angel-chorus rings;
The Shepherds, thro' the dusk, are drawing nigh;
St. Joseph's lantern glows.... The Eastern Kings
Stand out, like giants, 'gainst the bright'ning sky.
"*Glory to God!*"—(the swelling strains increase)
"*And, on the earth, to men of good-will—peace!*"

III.

"*A child is born to us, and a Son is given to us, and the government is upon his shoulders; and his name shall be called the Angel of great Council.*"—Isaias ix.

Within the Bethlehem of these poor hearts,
The manger of our souls, O Prince of men!
Come, in Thy pity, and be born again!—
Ere yet the golden Christmas-tide departs,
Love, with its thousand sweet and tender arts,
Shall emulate the Shepherds' glowing zeal,
Or, like the Magi from the Orient marts,
Shall gold, and myrrh, and frankincense reveal.

O Babe, so rich in Thy great poverty,
Give us Detachment's grand, divorcing grace!
O Babe, sublime in Thy humility,
Grant us, in Thee, all pride to self-abase!
O suff'ring Babe, so blissful in Thy woe,
A self-denying joy, on us, bestow!

The God-Man.

"Would I might be as God!" the first man cried,
When, with forbidden fruits, Sin's reign began.—
Lo! to repair the ruin wrought by Pride,
Christ, in the manger, we behold as Man!

Bethlehem's Queen.

"And going into the house, they found the Child with Mary, his Mother."—Matt. iii, 11.

O what would this life be without our sweet Mother?
—A desert divested of well-springs and trees,
A land without music, light, fragrance, or flowers,
A black, sultry night, without moonlight or breeze!

No solace for souls in their struggles with Satan,
No hope for the sinner engulf'd in despair,
No light for the saint in his doubts and temptations,
No stronghold of peace in a world full of care;

Dear *Cause of our joy!* bearing Bliss in thy bosom,
Clear *Mirror of justice!* resplendent with light,
Rare *Mystical Rose!* in thy glory a-blossom,
Fair *Star of the morning!* dispelling our night,—

Tho' all the foul fiends of the regions infernal

Assail the sad spirit with clamorous din;
Tho' earth and the earthy obscure the Eternal,
And Life's brightest promise be blighted by sin,—

What bliss but to feel the cool print of thy sandal
On fiery promptings and passions aglow;
To nestle, like birds, 'neath thy sky-color'd mantle,
And calm our hot hearts on thy bosom of snow!

What bliss thro' the darkness, the heat, and the clamor,
To fly to thy feet, to thy virginal shrine,—
And there, in thy presence, releas'd from Sin's glamor,
Drink in deepest draughts of thy spirit divine!

O drear would our life be without this fair Flower,
This Lily of Israel, blooming alone!
Sweet Christ! how we bless Thee for Bethlehem's dower,
Which made Thy pure Mother forever our own!

Milton Keynes UK
Ingram Content Group UK Ltd.
UKHW030627061024
449204UK00004B/243